From A WI

Manifestation

Brigette A. Ways Washington

Revised edition

I dedicate this book to my readers. May you be inspired to ignite the world with the love of God.

Acknowledgments

First and foremost, I give God all the glory and honor for what he has done and is doing in my life. For without him there is nothing that is possible and with him all things are possible.

I acknowledge my family and friends for their support.

Table of Contents

Man's Failure

The fall of man is the result of him believing
that his abilities are based on his own existence.
When in fact, his creation was a word. Spoken
by the Word, God himself. He engaged the
very dust that he created. Out of it became man,
a living soul. How often have we tripped and
stumbled causing us to miss or delay our call?

A Leader's Trail

A man who leads is challenged by his own
vision. Which may leave some wondering
where he is going. For his pace may be too
quick for them to understand.
However, their confusion is not his concern.
His only mission is to be out in front.
A true leader is motivated by the thought that
others will follow his guide. He exerts
patience for those that lag behind. Not being
condemned if they fail because the leader
will never lead them off his trail.

To Worship You

What a privilege it is to come before your greatness. You are the king of kings. You greet me even as the pauper that I am unworthy of your presence. My finite being cannot sufficiently describe who you are to me. Oh, to worship you!

YOU ARE......................

EL................................Mighty Strong Prominent
                                    Creator

EL -SHADDAI............. ..... All Sufficient

ADONAI........................ Master

JEHOVAH ....The Self Existent One

JEHOVAH JIREH...............Provider

JEHOVAH ROPHE............. .Healer

JEHOVAH NISSI............... .The Lord of Banner

JEHOVAH M'KADDESH. .... The Lord Who
                                    Sanctifies

JEHOVAH SHALOM.......... The Lord of Peace

                                    AMEN and SELAH

Less We Forget

We gleam with the pride of kings and queens.
Very aware that we are no longer the
characters of our past lives. And now, we have
little patience for those who speak otherwise.
Less we forget!
Our hearts rejoice over our redemption. We
purposely void those we left behind. We
walk past them, as we go to fellowship with
our new friends.
Less we forget!
Our hearts are filled with gladness but, we do
not share the key to obtaining this kind of joy.
Are we afraid? Do we think that it will be
taken away.
Less we forget!
We were once sinners too. It is only through
God's grace and mercy that we are saved. We
must go throughout the world to tell of His
good news.
Less We Forget!

New Mercies Everyday

I opened my eyes without any effort and was blessed
with the beauty of sunlight.
Then realized that my heart had not missed a beat.
It had completed its assignment without any
intervention from me.
I stood up with the mobility of my limbs. There were
no paralyzes preventing me from starting my day.
I ran to the kitchen quickly, solely concerned about
quenching my thirst.
Suddenly, the glass fell and there was a loud sound.
I looked at the shattered glass broken all around.
Staring, I was reminded of how God had kept me.
A broken and scattered mess, giving me the victory
over my test.
I repented for not thanking the Lord for making so
many ways, and the new mercies he gave me each
and every day.

My Oath

I look into this mirror and, I now understand.
What I see is a miracle. I was chosen to be
in-spite of my difficulties. My heart keeps
on beating, even when I feel like I cannot
breathe.
There is no other like me and I am
like no other. My distinction is not based on
my physical being. It is the divine purpose
assigned uniquely to me. This truth I will
forever believe. It in your word that I boast
and on it I will stand. This is my solemn
oath.

It's Harvest Time

Oh! What a time it is to reap. Cry out with
excitement.

Your wait for manifestation has arrived!

It is harvest time.

The planting of your seeds was not a painless
deed.

For it required that your flesh would die to
comfort and ease.

But you kept on with your chore.

The work had to be done.

You planted your seeds, empowered by the sun.

How else could your labor have been shown?

The evidence is in what you see that has grown.

Gather up what you have sown.

Bring out the wine It is harvest time!   .

More Than Just Ushers

Our assignment is far greater than just passing
out the church's programs.
We set the atmosphere upon the people entering
the house.
We represent our Lord and Savior Jesus Christ.
Exemplifying his spirit of love, making his
presence known to them.
Their coming back will be because they felt his
loving arms. As we embraced them at the door.

Still Praise Him!

The weight of life's toils has shaking up what appears to be your very foundation.

Still praise him!

The constant flow of debt appears to be suffocating you with heartaches and concerns.

Still praise him!

The enemy has seduced your family and friends with a spirit of strife.

Still praise him!

Your body is wrecked with pain and your strength is fading away.

Still praise him!

God's divine esteem is not predicated on our earthly circumstances. But our deliverance is predicated on the very perfume of our praise unto Him.

Let everything that have breath praise ye the Lord!

Dare To Venture

At what cost does a man dare to venture

beyond what is in front of him?

Is he willing to embrace what others cannot

see?

Will he stand firm against the darts of ridicule?

Will his vision lead him towards his destiny?

Or will he simply miss his season for fear of

him having to go it alone.

The Gift of Peace

My journey had been a long one. At times I felt
like there was no end in sight. The redness in my
eyes revealed the tears that I cried, during many
sleepless nights.
There was strife in my house. My money was tight
and my friends all left me left and right. As if I
had become their enemy.
And then I remembered, what God's word spoke to me.

Romans 5:1
Therefore, being justified by faith, we have peace
with God through our Lord Jesus Christ.

I thanked God for the victory, dried my tears and
closed my eyes. That night I slept indeed.
For I had been given the gift of God's peace.

Every Promise

Do not become entangled with all of the things of this world. For every promise of God shall come to pass. Break loose from a mindset of complacency and despair. Lift up your head, stick out your chest. Raise up your hands! Then scream. I am a child of the king of kings! He is able to deliver me!

God's Promises

Are Signed Sealed and

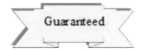

Guaranteed

Where Are All Of The Laborers?

Many gather together in awe of great possibilities but do
nothing to make them happen
Where are all the laborers?
There's no denying that the work needs to be done. A
multitude of idle words will not do anything. For the work
is not done and the land still lies broken and barren.
Where are all the laborers?

Look Forward

Yesterday is here but is now passing by. Look ahead for tomorrow is another day. In other words, today is nearing its end and the future will take its place. The significance of this new dawn is the evidence of encountering new experiences. Therefore, do not burn fuel over the old wonders of yesterday. Tomorrows wonders have not yet been seen. Only God knows what's coming our way.

Psalms 105:2

Sing unto him, sing psalms unto him: talk ye of all his wondrous works.

Zion's Choir

We will sing praises that permeate the atmosphere with the wonders of his glory. The sound of heaven shall soar from the depths of our souls. The God of our gifts will smile when we open our mouths.

Our assignment is not to entertain but to lift of the perfume of his praise. Healing will take place. . Deliverance will operate. Our songs will resemble the sound of the trumpet's ring.

GET UP!

Labor no more in pity. Wherefore is your faith?

Has he not shown you mercy every day?

Get up!

Why have you turned your focus? Is he not the

 one who has given your life?

Get up!

Do not die over the lack of things? God can and

will supply all of your needs.

Get Up!

Jesus Christ is our Lord, the risen king.

Get up!

It's More Than That

The world calls it plain ole luck Some say that it was done

by the hands of great minds.

Still others say that one's karma is what we should trust.

All lies!

Miracles, signs, and wonders is God's pleasures that he gives.

He spoke it and it came to be.

He speaks it and it is achieved.

Luck! Skills! Karma!

It's none of that.

This is the truth and unadulterated fact.

It's more than that!

F.L.E.S.H

Faith Lost Equals Spiritual Homicide

Our flesh was never created to have precedence over our minds. Let it not rule your actions. For in it, there lies your eternal tragedy. It occupies the lust of the eyes, the pride of life, and more. Power and control are the core of its allure

. It denounces faith, telling you to only believe in what you can see. Until you no longer look to God at all.

What comes after is your earthly demise.

This is the enemy's plan that so that you do not thrive

. Which ultimately causes your flesh to commit spiritual Homicide

Finally!

This thing had attached itself to me, like an outfit unable to be taken off. Its fit was uncomfortable. The smell of its constant wear became too much for me to bear. I struggled to pull on it, yank on it and even rip it apart. But my strength was weakened. It was too much for my heart.

So, I accepted what I thought was my destiny Crying, fearful and concerned that others could see what I was wearing upon me. Then one day as usual, I carried this thing. When a light so brightly lit transcended through me.

The more I looked to the sun (Son) the looser the hold came to be. I began to see me free, and off came one sleeve. I felt free, and off came the other sleeve. I was free! Dropping those things which had me bound. And today, I can say that I know that I am free. I am finally free!

To God be the glory for his son Jesus Christ, who with his power did cast down this thing.

I Knew!

Something had happened. I no longer desired to quench the hunger of my flesh. I started to tell a lie. As I had done in the past. But something held my lips in contrast.

Then I heard someone speak ill will of me. I ran to curse my enemy. I opened my mouth to speak of much harm.

Instead, I lifted up both my arms. I gave God the praise for what he had done. I had been changed through the blood of his only begotten son. And from that day I was never the same. I am a new creature in Jesus Christ. Thorough whose blood he paid the price

What great news! This I knew.

THIS JOURNEY…

Let us not forget that our present journey is about a temporary walk. For our predestined journey to eternity was prepaid by the lamb freely given by God. Don't weary yourself with the things of this land. Rest with the assurance of knowing that this journey will end, and a more glorious one will begin.

Get Ready! Get Set! Go!

On your mark! Be steadfast. This is not the time to give up.
The battle is already won. Your season has just begun.

Get ready! Preparation is the key to walk all over the enemy.

Prayer and fasting must precede you before stepping out. It
takes more than just a mere shout.

Get set! Receive your blessing. Do not let it pass you by. It
requires that you lower yourself.

It is all for God's glory. Which is more precious than silver
or gold.

Go! Run after it with everything that you have, your true
worship, your praise and undoubting faith.

Now know that this race was but a test to see if in him
you really trust.

On Your Mark! Get Ready! Get Set! Go!

True Love

We are born with an innate need to be loved, even from within the confines of the womb We thrive on it. A tender touch and a softly spoken word helps us to develop into a healthy baby boy or girl. Why is it that we need this thing? Some people die for it. Some will kill for it. And still, others lie for it. We are deeply consumed with having it. It is because we were created by love, who is love, with love.

Genesis 1:26

And God said, let us make man in our image, after our likeness.

John 3:16

For God so loved the world, that he gave his only begotten son.

If we would only realize that the gift of love was given to us freely. However, it can only be completely experienced when we connect with him who is the only true love.

The Sacrifice

There is nothing that we give without expecting
something in exchange.
We view it as a loss and tremble at the possibility
of coming out emptied handed.
It's unimaginable that one would suffer the punishment
for a crime that they had not committed.
We mortal beings would cry out. I'm innocent!
I'm not guilty! I didn't do it!
We would plead our case. Hoping to be vindicated
and another put in our place.
But our Lord and Savior Jesus Christ was willing to
pay that very price. For God, his father made him
the great sacrifice.

My Lord the King

The evidence of his uniqueness has nothing to do

with me. It is knowing that I am a child of the king.

My life is not my own and my purpose for living is to

serve him alone.

He who sits high on heaven's throne.

My steps are ordered when I consult in him, my Lord.

I thank him for choosing me

I look forward to seeing Jesus my king in eternity.

Savor Your Blessing

Savor your blessing. It was given to you before you
were. It had nothing to do with the sweat of your labor.
The work was done before your entrance into time. You
were given the blessing of eternity. It was and is yours
for the taken. Just believe that Jesus Christ died so that
you and I could be redeemed.

Oh, taste and see that the Lord is good!

When The Groom Arrives

At his arrival I pray that I hear his voice calling me into his
arms.

Let me not be caught being in a relationship with

the things of this world.

It will be of no essence to check for sin then.

For at his descending, it will be the end.

All of the work should have been done.

Let my report say that I have passed the test, and

then my Lord and Savior calls me his righteousness.

Oh! My holy and divine groom take me with you.

My spirit cries out!

This is what living saved is all about.

Seasons

Seasons come and they go. For their presence is but for a time.

Their assignment was pronounced before the foundations of

this earth. Each has a defining moment. Which will surely take

hold. Will you be ready when your season unfolds?

Cease it! It is a short visit. Don't waste time on irrelevant reports.

Recovering may cause your delay, causing your season to slip

away.

Is it your season?

It's A Personal Thing

It's not to be exposed to the world, although the

evidence of it will shine through. There is no

place for interruptions. The moment Is between

you and him.

Some may become jealous of the time that you

spend loving on him.

Discount them!

It is his pleasure that you are out to win.

The dialogue you have with your king of kings are

indeed, a personal thing.

Shhhhhhhhhhh….

The Unbearable Bearable

Catering to its attacks was not a choice. Although the sting of its targets was an unexpected surprise. Trouble came from every side. It appeared as if I was trapped.
I announced my retreat, proclaiming my defeat by the enemy's wicked deeds.
But then I remembered..........

Psalms 46:1
God is our refuge and strength, a very present help in trouble.

I used my praying tongue, lifted up my praising hands and, held firm to my faith in him.
I began to see me overcoming every obstacle.
In him I was and am triumphant.

The unbearable became bearable.
        To God Be the Glory

Lord! Remove This Struggle

I'm buckling under this pressure and I know that it is to

your divine displeasure.

I dare that I would forget all that you have done for me.

You have delivered me when I was bound.

Picked me up the many times that I have fell.

It is my heart's desire to do your will, but doubt keeps turning

Its ugly wheels. I know that this is not of you. God please!

It is futile to tussle and wrestle.

Lord remove me from this terrible struggle.

No Sense In Hating On It

Why despise me for the favor that I wear?
I had nothing to do with it.
I was just chosen.
It is said that favor is not fair.
Why ignore me when I call out your name?
Doing so, won't change this truth.
Favor is about God's power and not about
fleshly fame.
Praise the Lord with me.
When it's your turn, I'll praise the Lord for your victory.
We are his children.
Loved by the king, not spiritual enemies.
There is no sense in hating on it.
For favor is not something that you can earn.
It is our God's divine choosing to whom he
gives his precious gift.
There's no sense in hating on it.

What Love

There was or will never be such a great sacrifice.

He knew it was coming. Still, he hid not from this gruesome event.

Fear was no match for his

awesomeness.

It was as a fading raindrop. It had no place in his holiness.

This cross he had to bear.

How else could we have been truly redeemed?

He saw it. He took it. He obeyed it. His cause was his cross for our

crossing.

What Love.

It's A Heart Thing

It's a mystery of how it works. It does not function on emotions. Although one would think so. Its interaction is based on his word.

His word which tells us to pray for our enemies. Even when our minds tell us to take them down. We wonder why we cannot act on what we feel. Our permission to do otherwise is still denied. We can no longer do our own thing, as we are children of the king of kings. For with our God, it is a heart thing.

When God Speaks

When God speaks the very air that we breathe ceases to exist.

For it bows down to the presence of its king.

There is nothing that exceeds his greatness.

The very sun, the moon, the birds, and then there is us.

The only creation that God gave a soul to live holy and just.

What a privilege it is to hear his voice.

It's an indication that a relationship does exist.

Oh! Lord God. I pray that my ears will be attentive to what
you have to say.

My heart truly desires to remain humble and meek
to hear you God when you speak.

A Second Dance

I traveled through this journey seeking to accomplish the assignment for which I was created. However, my eyes had strayed beyond their designated course. My heart sought its own rule. I had become motivated by the desire of my flesh, which led me to an existence of confusion and doubt. Then the creator of my purpose, Jesus Christ, despite my failures allowed me the privilege of a second chance. Ole through your mercy, I have been allowed a second dance.

 Not Yet!

Not yet does not mean never. But it surmises

that waiting is the prerequisite before now can

come into existence.

First, one must believe that it is so, even when not

yet has been spoken in your ear.

Secondly, you have to have the faith to know that

it's already done.

And finally, one must be on constant alert and in

steady preparation.

For when now suddenly appears it will not destroy

or overwhelm you.

Then will you embrace what you already knew what

was going to take place in your life.

You're waiting has not been in vain!

TESTIFY

What do you do when life is taking you through?

Do you roll over in defeat and die? No!

You testify.

Testify about your Lord's goodness.

Allow your mind to revisit the mercy trips he extended

to you.

When your finances appear to be dwindling away do you

stop singing?

No! You humble yourself and pray and then shout out

with a victorious praise.

For in him we must understand that failure is not

recognized. So, keep your head to the sky and testify.

Again, I say testify until another soul comes running

nigh. Then he too will come to know

how to testify.

Beyond Feelings

It's not based on emotions, for emotions fluctuate.

It's not based on our own thoughts about a situation.

In them we will find limitations, confusion, and

chaos.

Which are all finite answers to our conditions.

How often are we misled when we rely on our

mortal sight?

A battle that we do not have to fight.

We were all sinners lifted by your grace and mercy,

transformed by the word of God. It is not by might,

nor by power but by his spirit says the Lord.

Ring out with singing.

This truth is beyond feelings.

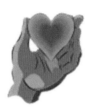

God's Divine Love!

He healed my body. Then I went on my way, never to think on it another day. I was hungry but had no money at all.

He came and made a way. I ate until I was left with food for days far away. I got up from my table, never giving him the praise. He gave me gifts. Which the world wanted to see. I strutted around as if it was all because of me.

Something happened, and it all came tumbling down.

There were none of my friends to be found. Feeling hopeless and lonely, I humbled myself. I cried out to Jesus Christ.

In him I had to trust. It was a must. Please forgive me I prayed.

Then I heard a voice so sweetly say, I forgive you are sounding from above . It was truly God's divine love.

Let Stuff Go!

We are consumed by its value and the heaviness of its weight.

Our whole focus is on maintaining it, and displaying it before

our friends. None of these things shall be seen at heaven's

gate. It becomes the purpose for us getting up each day. Why

do we give so much credence to these things?

They get in our way. Causing us to lose our spiritual wings.

Give him all the praise and it will remain yours to possess.

Then you will know to let stuff go.

Hear It! Believe it! Speak It! Do It! See It!

What good is a word if it has not been spoken? It's like a candlestick, never being exposed to flame. What good are instructions absent of listening ears.

It is useless to instruct those who refuse to hear. It requires that you extend yourself beyond the limits in front of you.

Push past the stagnation of the minute before. Eyes only able to focus on the circumstances of their time, will miss the possibility of a breakthrough being insight.

Blindness is not caused by the inability of the eyes to see.

It is the lack of the mind to conceive. A blind man who can see himself as a king, has more sight than a man, who is able to see and sees his life in terms of defeat.

Hear it! The voice of God is distinct from any other voice.

Believe It! His every word. Not one word will come back void.

Speak It! Say what God directs you to say.

He will direct your way.

Do it! For in obeying, you'll embrace your destiny.

See it! His many blessings are yours to receive.

Convicted!

I hid under the guise of a relationship. I called out his name but did not call on him. I clapped my hands like the others who gave him praise, having no real understanding for why my hands were raised. I read the Bible like a common book.

In truth, it was a mystery to me. I was not willing to study in order to get the victory.

I tried to remain comfortable in my turmoil but un- easiness was on my every side. The more I resisted, the more I drifted into a life of spiritual demise.

It was then that I confessed that I was not committed to living righteously. So, I humbled myself, fell on my knees.

Begging, God please! Deliver me.

Believing that God heard my prayer. This time it came from my heart. I called on my father, and now I have been set apart. My thoughts had been restricted to doing God's will. It did not feel good at the time of its visit, but I thank God for being truly convicted.

For God So Loved the World

We were not and he made us to become. Our nature was wretched, far from the of our King. We had nothing to offer. For all creations divinely he brought to be. There was no hammering, drilling, or a sketch instructing him on what to do. He spoke it and what was not, came on the scene. In the beginning was His word, which was Him and with Him obeyed Himself and caused whatever He decreed to those who believed In Him, there is no intrusion of His thoughts. For our finite minds cannot conceive, less in His word we are taught So, from the beginning he deemed a great sacrifice. Which was his son Jesus Christ. One who is human would ask. Why would someone pay such a great price. We are only people without any pearls, and the answer my friend is ……….

For God So Loved The World.

Born For Greatness

It was miraculous, your creation. For you were formed
meticulously by hands void of human errors. Your assignment
was ordered before your own birth. You see now that you have
purpose on this God's earth.

A man you were called and then given an assignment to
fulfill. Some have failed, stating that it was too much on
their plate.

Do not forget that when you were made, God's divine
hands took your burdens to bear.

So, my brother, my sister, dust off the residue of this life's miry
clay. God is gracious. Keep believing! It's through him that you
will find that you were born for greatness

Printed in Great Britain
by Amazon

10533444R00031